Law of Attraction to Make More Money

12 Hidden Truths to Help You Shift Your Mindset and Start Attracting the Abundance You Deserve
(without Trying So Hard)

By Elena G. Rivers

Copyright Elena G. Rivers © 2019

www.loaforsuccess.com

All rights reserved. No part of this publication may be reproduced, stored in a retrieval system, or transmitted, in any form or by any means, electronic, mechanical, photocopying, recording or otherwise, without the prior written permission of the author and the publishers.

The scanning, uploading, and distribution of this book via the Internet or via any other means without the permission of the author is illegal and punishable by law. Please purchase only authorized electronic editions, and do not participate in or encourage electronic piracy of copyrighted materials.

Elena G. Rivers © Copyright 2019 - All rights reserved.

Legal Notice:

This book is copyright protected. It for personal use only.

Disclaimer Notice:

Please note the information contained in this document is for educational and entertainment purposes only. Every attempt has been made to provide accurate, up to date and completely reliable information. No warranties of any kind are expressed or implied.

Readers acknowledge that the author is not engaging in the rendering of legal, financial, medical or professional advice. By reading this document, the reader agrees that under no circumstances are we responsible for any losses, direct or indirect, which are incurred as a result of the use of information contained within this document, including, but not limited to, errors, omissions, or inaccuracies.

Contents

Introduction 5

A Special Offer from Elena to Help You Manifest Faster. 21

Mindset Shift #1 Is Your Desire Good for You? 23

Mindset Shift #2 Grow Your "No" Muscle 35

Mindset Shift #3 The Biggest Mistake Behind Finding Your *Why* . 42

Mindset Shift #4 The LOA KISS Method 56

Mindset Shift #5 The Most Powerful Word for a Bad Day (aka Your Manifestation Bridge) 58

Mindset Shift #6 Own Yourself 73

Mindset Shift #7 The Resourceful Method 81

Mindset Shift #8 Your LOA Stamina to Keep Believing 85

Mindset Shift #9 Abundant Mindset Mastery 88

Mindset Shift #10 Be on the Other Side 92

Mindset Shift #11 The Invisible Force That Makes You Fail or Succeed (and how to use it to manifest what you want) 94

Mindset Shift #12 Your Net Worth Starts with Self-Worth 96

A Special Offer from Elena to Help You Manifest Faster. 100

Introduction

If you have ever tried to use LOA to make more money but found yourself frustrated and with few or no results, you have come to the right place.

Perhaps you have read other books, taken courses and tried everything under the sun, including affirmations, meditations and visualizations.

You have seen other people on the same journey get results and you were wondering what you are doing wrong.

If that's how you're feeling right now, don't worry, I have some good news for you.

Believe it or not, I have been in the same situation.

Not only that, but I have invested tens of thousands of dollars both in courses and mentorship related to the Law of Attraction and Spirituality as well as Self Help and Business.

I have experienced lots of failure and frustration in my life, and it was only on my 42nd birthday that I began to change my life.

You see on that day, my 42nd birthday, quite by accident, I met a mentor, a mindset mentor who was able to help me.

I did not expect that day to change my life at all. In fact, it was my birthday and I was feeling so depressed.

I had been through a tough divorce. I had lost my job. I had been diagnosed with adrenal exhaustion and had to start taking medication. I was putting on weight. I was living off my savings and doing some freelance design work on side. I was simply getting by. That day, my 42th birthday, I didn't feel like seeing anyone.

All my friends were married.

Showing off their children and loving, caring husbands.

Some of my female friends chose to live a different lifestyle and have corporate or entrepreneurial careers while enjoying frequent vacations in exotic locations. Showing off their healthy fit bodies, enjoying great friendships, getting affluent clients and huge appreciation for what they were doing.

Some of my friends were successfully living off their passion and art.

In other words, they all seemed happy and successful. Yet it seemed like I was the hardest working one. The one who invested so much money in courses and mentors. With zero results. So frustrating.

Little did I know that it was meant to happen.

It was a part of my journey, as you will later see through this very book. All those years of pain and rejection. Working hard and studying from different mentors eventually exploded into a life I am blessed to be living today.

That is why I am writing this book. I believe that everyone deserves to have this information and that flow of abundance. Not only financial abundance, but also an abundance that spreads and circulates to other areas of life. That may sound a bit woo-woo to some of you. I get that. I used to be very skeptical about everything. I will tell you this- this book is more science and mindset that will help you use LOA to your advantage.

This is exactly what happened to me...

So...on my 42nd birthday, I had nothing to show for.

My plan was to get drunk all by myself while watching TV. A typical night for me at that time.

I was absolutely fine with that as I had lost hope.

I had moved to a smaller and cheaper apartment, the cheapest I could get. I was counting every penny. Honestly, I did not even have the money to invite friends over. I just wanted to be all by myself and cry. I felt so numb so lost, it was like I didn't even feel my body anymore.

I was in so much mental and emotional pain that even the mere thought of picking up a spiritual or self-help book or watching a LOA video would make me cry. I would think:

Why are the creators of those materials successful and I am not? Why it's working for them but not for me?

In the morning, I did my super-cheap shopping...and yeah, I had that plan to stick to...go back home, drink cheap wine and just hope everyone would forget about me and my birthday. I didn't want anyone to ask about me. I had lost contact with most of my friends and family anyway and they all thought I was a loser.

1. I lost my job.
2. My ex-husband was cheating on me with another woman.
3. I felt scammed. I had purchased so many courses that had promised me a better future. Both LOA as well as business courses. Nothing had worked. I no longer felt like learning and investing in myself and wanted to go completely offline. Whenever I would switch on my social media accounts, I would just see other people who were happy and successful, and it was very painful for me. I could not take it anymore. I feel very ashamed to admit it now, but I did have some suicidal thoughts during that period of my life. I was questioning the meaning of life and everything.

4. I had put on weight and felt moody and ugly. I had been diagnosed with a disease that, as all the doctors would tell me, required medication and strong hormonal therapy until the end of my life. That would affect my emotions and make me put on weight. I felt lost and confused, I didn't even feel like myself anymore. Friends and family suggested I get a boyfriend, but I just felt like staying at home.

I was thinking, *Man...if I could only afford to fly to another country and just stay there. Detach myself from the past. Disappear. Start all over again.*

So, on that particular day I was just about to switch off my phone when I received a call from a cousin of mine. A cousin I haven't seen in, like, fifteen years. He lived abroad in tropical countries. And yeah, he would always call or text on my birthday.

So, he called me and asked, "Hey, how are you? Guess what? I am going on a quick conference near your town. A friend of mine got sick and he transferred his ticket to me. It's a three hour drive from the hotel I am staying at, but it's not a problem at all. I really wanna see you. After the conference I can drive to your place or we can meet up somewhere. I am with some friends, they are very cool people, what do you say?"

Needless to say, it took some time for him to convince me.

As kids we always used to play around and had a good connection even without words.

His mom is my stepdad's sister, but I was raised by my stepdad. I never even met my dad. So, we were always like a family. Cousins.

My stepdad was always very into the system (get a degree, get a job, marry and have kids), however, his sister was more like a hippie and had brought up their kids in a different way. I always wondered how my cousin could afford to travel all the time and meet all those cool people.

Long story short, we decided to meet in a small bar at the town center. I forced myself to go there with a smile on my face.

When I arrived there and saw my cousin, I just felt like crying, which is what I did. I explained how I felt and I couldn't stop crying.

He said that the friend he was with for the conference was a mindset coach. He added, "I think he may be able to help you work through the issues you are feeling now."

I said, "Mindset coach? How will that help me? I need a career coach, a relationship coach and a health coach."

But, after a few drinks, I was like, "OK, let's see what he can do." I really had nothing to lose.

So there appeared Mr. Mindset coach. At first, I was thinking he would try to sell me his service or program, but he didn't. Yet, I really felt like it would be amazing if he could offer me some coaching.

I really got a lot of value from what he told me and our conversation kept on for hours and hours,

It all came down to a very simple pattern around my mindset and my perception. Eventually, I decided to invest in his coaching even though, knowing about my poor financial situation, he didn't want to charge me.

But I had this feeling...*Elena...this time you will invest in yourself and it will be different. You will take action. Things will change.*

He told me that my self-image wasn't really matching the goals I wanted to achieve along with many other things that came as a result of our improvised session at the bar.

From then on, we ended up working together, and through this inner work that I did my life was forever transformed.

Finally, I was able to distill the best information and divide it into powerful mindset steps that you too can do to start making more money. Whether it's through your job, business, other ventures or something unexpected.

Also, if you are already familiar with what I like to call traditional LOA techniques, whether it's old school LOA (classic visualizations, affirmations and meditations), or you are more on a New School jump wagon (here I refer to the Reality Transurfing school of thought), this book will help you shift your mindset and that will allow you take any LOA action from a totally different angle. The angle of being the boss, the owner, the producer of your life and never worry about being a victim.

I can assure you that it's a fresh approach, and if you are coachable and willing to change (aka become the most empowered and divine version of yourself) then this book will help you.

In fact, if you read it with attention and start analyzing patterns from your own life, you may start manifesting from a completely new perspective as soon as you start reading this book.

Some people may want to read this book several times. It's a short read so there should be no, "But I don't have the time" excuses.

Some people may want to focus on one specific step for longer. It all depends on you and your vision.

While reading, please don't judge yourself.

Be an observer of your own reality. Use constructive self-criticism rather than judgment. Some truths may be a bit painful. However, every transformation requires change.

That is how I view my life now and I was really at rock bottom.

Now, I don't like bragging about my income and I like to protect my privacy. It's something I really resonated with after reading the book *The Reality Transurfing*. Just like the author of that book states, he achieved certain levels of success but is not planning to show it off as it could affect his privacy and flow. I feel exactly the same way.

However, I can tell you this. I was able to triple my income within three months of using the strategies I developed after working with a mindset coach. Then, I tripled it again.

I was able to move abroad and change my environment too. I still ask myself, *how did it happen*?

Currently I am using a similar system to help people transform their health and love life too. However, money is not evil. Not at all. It's freedom and abundance you deserve, and I will show you the best and ethical mindset hacks to help you transcend your current situation.

An interesting fact- after diving into and internalizing the 12 mindsets I am sharing in this book, I was able to go back to the books and programs I invested in earlier and have success with them.

It all made sense to me and I felt like part of a bigger system designed for my needs and vision. Many of my friends and confidential mentees had the same experience. Especially my mentees who are in business. Suddenly after going through the 12 mindset shifts discussed here, they were able to successfully apply the information they had invested in previously.

In my case, I was able to go back to dozens of LOA and quantum physics courses I have taken and books I have read and make them work for me.

However, in alignment with what I have previously mentioned...it's not how many books you read, how many courses you take and how many seminars you attend.

It's not even how much action you take or don't take after going through the materials you study.

It's about how you take them.

While most LOA enthusiasts would say, "Ah, right, it's about the state you're in and your energy", what I want to show you through this book is there is much more to that. Yes, your energy is also very important, and I have written a few books related to LOA that focus mostly on your energy to help you manifest faster.

However, this book relates mostly to your mindset because that can affect your energy too.

One thing I have always been curious about is why there are people who don't really meditate. Yet they always manifest! They've never studied LOA yet they do something that allows them to manifest. How is it that whatever they put their hands on is a success?

It wasn't until I met my mindset coach that I began working through the issues that were stopping me not only from success but also from taking advantage of the numerous LOA resources I had studied. (These are proven to work because they have worked for many other people.)

It's very important that you don't just read passively. Even before we start diving into the tools, I want to teach you that you must have a curious mindset and do whatever it takes to be excited.

This isn't a book based on plain gratitude (although gratitude is extremely important).

It's all about deep transformation and stepping into the more empowered version of yourself that will allow you to create the life you deserve. In many cases you may even realize that you have not been able to manifest certain things as they were not really for you anyway and would not have made you happy. That can be a massive relief if you ask me, and it leads to replacing self-guilt and frustration with gratitude.

The strategies from this book have been designed specifically for the finance area of your life. Still, the mindset shifts and mechanisms I will teach you can also be applied to other areas of your life and can help you become what I like to call a manifesting high performer on your own terms. By tapping into your unlimited potential, you will be an inspiration to your loved ones. It is my deep desire that you internalize my teachings by applying them to your life so that you start getting results. Then, you can use your experience and knowledge to help other people too.

I believe in abundance not scarcity. If everyone followed the mindset shifts outlined in this book, the world would be an amazing place. There would be a flow of abundance, no complaining and everyone would just be happier.

While it would be childish of me to believe that such a collective shift could happen overnight, I believe in the compound effect, both on an individual as well as on a collective level.

So please, share this book and the teachings in it.

I am not on social media, and I don't have a podcast or a YouTube channel. I have nothing against people who use all those channels that modern technology offers. However, I know myself well enough to understand where I need to put my energy so that I can be effective in my mission and passion- helping people transform with what I have learned from LOA, all in a very practical and doable way, using one of the most popular mediums of learning- books.

I am blessed to be making a living from my passion which is art and design and I am also grateful that I get enough free time to pursue my writing career and my blog: www.LOAforsuccess.com which makes me feel whole and complete. This is my channel of expression. This is where I am good at teaching and sharing.

It allows me to share my stories and lessons learned with other people without affecting my flow and making me feel unfocused and even shattered like most of the social media channels I tried did.

For me, it's always been a passion to help others and express myself through my art as well as writing.

For you, it may be something different. I truly believe you will be able to discover your passion and tap into the flow of financial abundance by getting rid of emotional blocks that are holding you back. You will also eliminate what I like to call *LOA Short-Sightedness*. This is something that accounts for the fact that so many people give up and reject LOA as a concept that doesn't work for them.

Just like I don't do social media in order to be able to put my energy where I need to put it to be able to shine and help others shine, I do not organize any workshops or courses, although I know many people who do, and there is nothing wrong with that. They are very good at what they do. It's a good path for them and many people need to invest a lot of money in themselves to be motivated to apply the information they learned. That was my case.

Again, there is nothing wrong with that. I invested tens of thousands of dollars into both LOA, mindset as well as professional courses related to my passion and now career (art and design).

Whatever your situation is, this book will "unstuck "you and will get you on the right track. I can't wait to receive an email or review from you and witness your transformation on this journey with the system I will be sharing with you.

There are different ways to use this book, depending on your time and lifestyle:

Option #1 Read it in one sitting. Then, re-read each section and do the exercises.

Option #2 Assign a day for one mindset shift and after reading through each section, do the exercise. After twelve days (that is going through the twelve mindset shifts) evaluate and ask yourself which shift is the most important for you at this stage.

In case you get stuck, please don't hesitate to email me.

In order to email me, be sure to join my newsletter:

www.loaforsuccess.com/newsletter

Then, reply to the first email I send you and let me know if you have any questions.

Please note, this is my personal email and it's not handled by my assistant.

That is why it's really the best way to keep in touch with me and share your experiences.

Now, back to the book- I highly recommend that you focus on just a few mindset shifts you believe are the most important for you.

How will you know?

Ask yourself – when thinking about the new me with this new mindset, do I feel lighter and more excited? Would that help me change my life and manifest faster?

If the answer is *yes*, focus more on those.

Now- time to take some meaningful action here to help you transform!

Let's do this!

Thank you for taking an interest in this book. I truly believe it has the power to change your life.

Before we dive into the mindset shifts, be sure to read through the next page as I have a free newsletter & surprise gift that I am offering. When combined with the teachings shared in this book, you will be given the advantage that will make everyone around you wonder what it is that you are doing.

See you on the next page.

A Special Offer from Elena to Help You Manifest Faster.

The best way to get in touch with me is by joining my free email newsletter.

You can easily do it in a few seconds by visiting our private website at:

www.Loaforsuccess.com/newsletter

The best part?

When you sign up, you will instantly receive a free copy of an exclusive LOA Workbook that will help you raise your vibration in 5 days or less:

You will also be the first one to learn about my new releases, bonuses and other valuable resources to help you on your journey.

Sign up now and I'll "see you" in the first email.

Love,

Elena

Mindset Shift #1 Is Your Desire Good for You?

If you have ever consumed any success, self-help, business, high performance of even classical LOA materials, you probably already know that in order to be successful with your goals, you need to know what you want.

It's not hard to make a vision board.

It's not hard to write down what you want.

And it's not hard to record what you want and turn your desires into affirmations and meditations.

All the above-mentioned techniques are amazing if you actually know what you want, and it comes from you, from your core.

The problem? Most people don't know what they really want, even if they intellectually think they do. Very often people get into spirituality and LOA because they are looking for something else out there. Maybe they got burned out in their corporate jobs, or careers. Or maybe they spent years trying to achieve their goals and when they did, they ended up feeling miserable and unhappy.

The same question appeared: Was it worth it?

So how do you become clear on what you want? How will you know whether what you want comes from yourself?

First of all, you need to be very careful about what you put into your mind.

Then, you also need to accept what I like to call "temporary chaos". You don't need to have it all figured out in five seconds.

The #1 mistake that most people make with LOA is that instead of diving deeply into this step, they create their vision really fast, without even checking if that vision truly comes from their hearts.

Then, they try hard to manifest. Another mistake. Trying too hard sends the following signal to the Universe: "I don't have it, it's not for me, I need to work harder because I don't have it".

Then, there is frustration: "I can't manifest. Maybe I am not worthy. Let's try another course. Anyone up for a new guru and their secret methods?"

And again, no matter how good the next course is, without clear vision we can easily get lost.

My number one recommendation when it comes to creating your vision is this:

Take a weekend off. Only you. Book a hotel you have never been to, drive to another city or go somewhere unknown. Ideally, you would want a solo vacation for seven days, but that may be not doable for most people. That is why two days may be a good solution to start off with.

Another thing to optimize your efforts with, again are your vision and your core exercise. And yes, you can always change your vision and what not, that is fine, but why not dive deep now and get it right from the get-go?

Think about it. By constantly changing your mind, you are only confusing the Universe. Especially when it comes to your financial goals. These goals make most people add a ton of emotion and stress, because most people associate money with a lack of money and therefore stress, and not feeling worthy.

It should rather be associated with offering value, living your passion, creating a life of freedom and becoming a more empowered version of yourself which is amazing.

But... it all starts with focus. Very clearly defined vision that is detailed but attached to one specific transformation you are looking to achieve. You also need to remember that what you want already exists. It's not that you are creating it. It already exists just like the more empowered version of yourself exists too. It's a different reality and you need to apply this mindset- I simply need to tune it with my thoughts, actions and energy.

One of my early mistakes with LOA was that out of fear, I created a dozen of different vision boards that did not really connect to the same vision. Different vision boards with different houses and lifestyles.

I was thinking that any of them would be good for me. I guessed that by doing a shotgun approach I would at least be able to manifest something. Eventually something will materialize?

Wrong, wrong, wrong! A shotgun approach to manifesting will only make you burn out. A sniper approach works so much better, more on that later in this book.

Not surprisingly, during that time, I tried different business ventures. All of them failed. I invested a ton of money and never made any money. I could never commit to one idea.

Instead of creating one business, one client base and one strong asset, I was jumping all over the place. Thinking- *well, something will work eventually.*

(Oh, and I will also tell you this- I tried the same with diets and nothing worked. I could not lose weight, even though most of my vision boards had pictures of slim models and women that looked exactly the way I wanted to look.)

To make it worse I would journal every day. What Elena? But journaling is good, isn't it? Yes, it is, if you do it the right way.

But in my case...oh boy. I would just randomly add a ton of different goals and tried to visualize a bit of everything.

Now when it comes to creating your LOA abundance vision and manifest the income level you want, the focus you need to adopt is the same kind of focus that the best business people apply. Don't diversify too early and focus on creating strong assets. Better to have fewer assets but strong ones. You want assets that will work for you. In our case, assets that will lead to our ultimate manifestations that leave us speechless. How is that even possible?

In my career, I was blessed to work with very successful entrepreneurs (we are talking seven to eight-figure level entrepreneurs). They all told me the same thing. Most of them used to be stuck at the same income level. The money that would just allow them to pay the bills, business expense and taxes. They suffered because they could not grow, have the impact they wanted and have the sense of freedom and security that their businesses would not only survive but also thrive and change the world.

Their stagnation was due to the shotgun approach. Too many different projects and ventures, in the hope that something would take off. After all, the more the better, right? Why not diversify?

The more I studied money, and the law of attraction, the more patterns I saw. There are certain rules of both meaningful entrepreneurship/successful career and quantum physics that are basically the same. It's just that the human brain interprets them in a different way. The law is very simple- <u>the less you focus on the better</u>. Then you give it your full attention and it's really amazing!

Think about it…certain companies don't like employees who get a second job at their competitor company.

In my case, I used to run two unrelated businesses where I was trying to serve two different groups of people. It felt as if nobody would trust me because they didn't see me as an expert. Instead they saw me as someone who "tries to get their money" by doing a bit of everything.

Bad idea.

So…I started working with the mindset coach and got rid of the limiting belief that I am not good enough. I also stopped creating a ton of different vision boards and a ton of weak assets in the hope that something eventually would work. I just used to believe I wasn't at all worthy.

The moment I learned about my limiting beliefs, I was able to change my vision.

Like mentioned in my suggestions above, I booked a hotel in a new town for a few days. I disconnected from the internet.

I was all by myself in silence and spending lots of time in nature. I gave my brain a rest. I wasn't reading anything or listening to anything.

It was just me and my notebook.

Taking deep notes from my heart.

No stimulants, no caffeine. No alcohol. I also gave myself some time to meditate, get a massage, and eat healthy plant-based foods while also drinking fresh juices and clean water.

First two days I still didn't know exactly what I wanted. I had so much going on in my mind.

But I knew one thing- I had to focus on ME.

What would make ME happy.

ME. My feelings and my emotions. Not what I want or my desires.

You see, what you want is really a reflection of your feelings and emotions. Most people don't focus on their core but instead they just jump straight to creating a vision board. Using what I like to call a "rat race strategy".

Ok, lemme see. The Joneses got a new car, so let me go on Pinterest and find something and put it on my vision board and manifest it.

There is nothing wrong with wanting to have a nice car, I also like nice things. The question is- do you really care about that car? Maybe what you are really looking for is sense of freedom and wealth? Knowing that you have enough to get a nice "toy" when you please? But at the same not being too attached to it?

A former client of mine had a vision board with a beach house on it. I asked her, "Why did you put it there, how do you feel about it?"

She said, "Well, I guess my parents would like it."

I asked, "What makes you think so?

She said, "Because it's a house of someone who is successful and has a secure career. My parents would be proud of me if I had such a house."

Can you see where it's going?

After a deep talk we realized that she didn't even care about such a house. What she really cared about was establishing a stronger bond with her family and feeling accepted for who she is.

Keep asking yourself:

-Why?

-Why do I want it?

-How does it make me feel?

The second round of questions is:

-Does it make me feel light?

-Does it make me feel heavy?

In most cases, when you start off feeling heavy that vision is not your vision but someone else's. Other people may be quick at manifesting it, and maybe you thought you "could try too". Yes, you could, but is it right for you?

A friend of mine had different travel boards in her apartment. However, after a deep talk she realized that she wasn't really passionate about traveling but since many of her friends traveled a lot and knew a lot about different cultures and languages, she felt a bit unworthy. She felt that her knowledge about all those countries they would talk about was close to zero. She felt out of tribe.

But honestly, she had no passion for it while on the other hand her friends were very passionate about languages and traveling.

What she really wanted was to feel appreciated and that she was an expert at something. She just liked spending time with friends in her local area and would always be the last one to leave a bar while helping those who were going through relationship problems.

Today, that woman is a very well-paid relationship coach.

After diving deep, she changed her vision boards and aligned them more with her goals and visions instead of her friends'.

She kept visualizing the joy she would feel after helping people with their dating and relationship issues. She imagined getting "thank you" emails and text messages from people.

Finally, she decided to go all in to become an actual relationship coach. To this day she hates traveling! She loves connecting with her clients in person, in local cafes and bars. She has no problem attracting affluent clients and is creating a strong manifestation momentum really doing what she loves instead of just trying to chase other people's dreams.

Another former client of mine had vision boards of famous entrepreneurs and he thought he wanted to be like them. He tried so many businesses repeatedly. Why did he do it?

One of the reasons was that he thought that being an entrepreneur means you get famous and go on different podcasts and travel the world while meeting people. He also wanted to make money. However, once he learned how lonely entrepreneurship can get and about the sacrifices he would have to make, he realized that what would really make him happy was becoming an actor. He did. He gets to travel a lot, be interviewed on shows and he makes great money too. His first vehicle- entrepreneurship- did not really align with his vision but he had mistakenly believed that was his only way, to success.

After connecting with his emotions, he realized that he needed to change the vehicle as he was really spinning his wheels pursuing other people's dreams.

So, here's the task for you:

-Allow yourself some time off and get connected to your true feelings and emotions.

-Start off by asking yourself what would make you happy. Materialistic goals are fine if they are coming from you because you feel joy while being surrounded by the objects you want to manifest. However, if the root of your goal comes from insecurity and not feeling worthy or trying to impress the Jones' then I recommend you redefine your vision.

-After you have built those fundamentals in your imagination, set the intention to create a very simple and basic vision board, with just a few basic images that will not confuse your conscious and subconscious mind.

-Does it make you feel lighter or heavier? Of course, lighter should be the answer.

-Take care of your emotional state. Have an Epsom salt bath or get a massage if you have been having a stressful day. It's hard to align yourself with your vision if you're feeling stressed out and there is no point in creating vision board just for the sake of doing it.

Mindset Shift #2 Grow Your "No" Muscle

After going through the first step and creating your new, simple yet revamped vision board, you will know what to focus on in terms of people and opportunities.

After that first step, most entrepreneurs I know get rid of certain projects to be able to focus on the one thing that truly aligns with their vision and passion.

People who seek a more exciting career opportunity suddenly get clarity about which company to submit their CV too.

Action doesn't feel like action because you are not forcing anything. It doesn't feel like hustle or hard work. It feels good and you are taking it from the place of abundance and confidence that you and your vision are one.

Suddenly you feel energized and empowered.

One of the early mistakes I made with LOA was the classical, "Let me just think about it and it will happen" mistake.

What I mean by that is that some people believe that it's enough to think and what they think about is just something random circumstance or object they wish they could manifest but nothing ever happens. As you already know, one of the reasons is because it wasn't truly theirs in the first place and deep inside, they don't care about it or think it will help them get rid of their insecurities. (Mindset work that we do here in this book will help you shift many of those insecurities and limiting beliefs so have no fear, my friend, I am with you.)

Another reason that it fails is that they think about what they want, but they act from a place of lack and scarcity. Because of that they soon lose motivation and don't do anything.

The best way to manifest is by what I like to call the Fused Alignment Method:

1. Your vision is your own and makes you feel lighter and super-happy.
2. You center your mindset around this belief, please repeat after me: *What I want already exists and I take a meaningful action to fuse myself with my vision and I love it.*
3. You take care of your energy and focus. The Universe is putting you to the test....
4. You take action in a powerful and meaningful way. Just don't do a mad shotgun approach, it will only spread your energy too thin. Instead feel like a powerful designer of your life. Maintain singular focus.
5. Let your emotions guide you. Listen to your gut. Are you making another logical decision? Because, you know, it makes sense and is the next step that you feel you are

supposed to take? Do you feel as if it is being expected of you? Remember- if you're feeling heavy, and it doesn't feel right, chances are you are pushing your manifestations and deep desires away.

6. Learn to say *no* – when you decide to transform and to shift your mindset, you really need to control your mind and be very mindful of your time. That is why you need to learn to say *no* to people. Ask yourself, *can I afford it?* Your time is very valuable especially now that you are embarking on this new journey that later will allow you to help other people too. (Trust me, when you master the process I am teaching you thought this book, you really will feel like sharing it with other people.)

You want to be proactive and promise yourself to take care of your energy and focus. You really need to help yourself first.

Now, let's carry on…I know what you're thinking…

"Oh, Elena, but I still don't know how to manifest more money."

That's the thing…you need to let go of that thought for now.

For now, you need to focus on the clarity and vision.

It may come as you read this book a few more times.

You can empower yourself by controlling your time, focus and energy.

Simple example- I am a writer. I help and inspire people through the writing channel of creative self-expression.

I very often get asked by other writers, "Elena, how do you get ideas?" or "Elena, how do you get rid of writers' block?"

My answer is simple. I set an intention.

I never know exactly what I am gonna write, I just feel it.

I am not in the mindset of just sharing some information. I am in the mindset of providing you with tools for your transformation.

When I write, I manifest by creating, but that creation comes naturally. I don't need to try hard. Some may call it a *flow* or a *zen* state of mind. I am in motion. That motion helps me manifest. I forget about me and my desires and myself. I just focus on writing. I am aligned, and it feels like I am nowhere, but I am also somewhere. It just flows.

I did used to struggle with so-called writers' block. A negative review or a hate email would affect me and my writing.

Then, after doing some inner work, I began noticing patterns. Our minds very often repeat what we have learned through an environment that shaped us. So, for example, in the case of my writing, I remembered that the first lesson I ever got, the teacher would talk about the writer's block all the time and so did other writers. Because of that, I was in a mindset of "it's normal to feel blocked, all writers do".

Then I realized that it was not empowering me or my message.

And I made a new decision**: I have a writer's flow.**

So, I basically swapped *block* with *flow*. It has served me very well.

I focused on the bigger picture and on my mission. A part of me detaches from my writing so that I can transfer all my energy into the message that I am sharing. It's a very liberating flow and something that can be achieved in all areas of life. In fact, this book will guide you on how.

Why does it flow for me? I am not a talented writer. My vocabulary is basic, and I need an editor who heals my grammar when needed to make sure I create a quality product.

But I take care of my focus and energy and I am proactive.

I disconnect from the outer world and social media.

First of all, if my preferred channel of expression is writing books that can help you on your journey, I stick to that. I know people who organize workshops and that's great. Some people create a webinar and then offer coaching or a course, and that is fine too.

Imagine though if I tried to do all of it at once. I would not be aligned. I know people whose favorite form of self-expression is video or a podcast. For me, it's writing so I stick to that and I say *no* to anything else.

Also, every day I get some offer or other from a digital marketing company wanting to help me with this or that, but I don't want to lose my focus. People who find me through my books naturally enjoy this format of consuming content. It's as simple as that.

Same with health and fitness. I don't do any complicated diets. I eat a clean, mostly plant-based diet.

I jog every morning, five times a week and then I do yoga. That's it. I don't overcomplicate things as it would make me lose my focus. I would feel too stressed out with things I have to do.

And now I just focus on what I do, and it is my second nature.

The point of this is- learn to say *no* to things, circumstances and even people who do not align with your vision. You can still be kind and nice. There's no need to be arrogant as that's bad energy.

I usually say *no* with, "Dear...thanks for your offer. I really appreciate your time. As much as I would like to help, currently

I need to stay focused on the projects I have already committed myself to. I am sure you will do amazingly well anyway. Love, Elena".

Mindset Shift #3 The Biggest Mistake Behind Finding Your *Why*

You have probably heard many self-help gurus talk about the importance of *why*. And yeah, it's totally true, but most people miss this point just like they miss the point of a truly aligned vision board.

So how to find your *why* specifically for the purpose of manifesting more money and abundance?

How to get in a state of mind that will allow you to create your own template? So that with that template you can not only maintain your increased income but also keep manifesting more and more while feeling fulfilled.

The best exercise you can do is to think about your current income goal. Also, for most people, I would start off by doubling your current income as your goal. Not that I don't believe in unlimited abundance or tapping into your true potential. It's just that for most people coming up with huge goals when it comes to their income usually eliminates all their manifestations as their subconscious mind just doesn't get what is going on.

For example, if a person makes a minimum wage and sets a goal of making 1 million dollars a month, it's just a number and a goal. Your mind can't fully comprehend it, and not only your subconscious mind but even your conscious mind goes like- *ok time to go back to earth, this is not for me.*

And that makes you go back to the same old, same old. No matter how many millionaire vision boards or visualizations or affirmations you produce, your inner mechanism will rebel against this number.

That is why as a general rule I would start off with a goal that is your current income multiplied by two. In some cases, you can make your current income tripled as your goal.

Is that it?

Nope. Because again your mind doesn't care about the numbers.

It cares about the feelings and experiences and about you already feeling as if you were in that reality. The trick? You must feel that way at least 80% of time. That is why you need to be aware of any negative voices, fear or self-doubt.

Your brain will try to put you off even setting your manifestation goal. The classical ways of it include making you look for excuses like:

-Oh, but when I make more money, I am gonna have to pay more taxes and get an accountant and that will be expensive.

- BOOM- a scarcity mindset sneaks in and you are basically done.

So here is the exact process I have used myself and I am always using to reach the new levels in my manifestations. Manifestation may take time. If it takes longer than you expected, the trick is to stick to your vision. Do not allow your behavior or negative thoughts pull you off track. Staying on track should not feel like a chore either.

1. First, you set a simple income goal. For example: your current income is 5 k a month and your goal is 10 k a month.
2. Now, since your mind doesn't really get the difference between those numbers, you want to take another approach. This is what I like to call Perfect Manifestation Fusion Method.
3. The Perfect Manifestation Fusion Method requires that you place all your focus on the experiences and feelings that earning 10 k a month and therefore doubling your income will give you.
4. As you go through this process remind yourself to be aware of all the negative patterns and self-sabotage that will sneak in. In case you find yourself with any negative thoughts that tell you are not worthy or deserving, make sure you spot the pattern and re-frame it.

For example:

Limiting belief:

But if I make more money, my friends will leave me.

New, empowering belief that will help you manifest faster:

My friends will be inspired by me. I will be able to help and support those around me. I am very grateful for who I am becoming.

Same with- *Oh, but I will need an accountant and it will be very complicated and taxes are expensive in my country.*

New belief:
There is always a solution and I deserve to be making 10 k a month or more. I believe in the flow of abundance. As I manifest more and more abundance, I spread it around by hiring people who offer me their help.

Or:
My new income is aligned to the new me who I am becoming right here, right now. The new me already

> *exists and will take me to a new place a new country where I will be able to enjoy more abundance freely.*

You see, you may be stuck in your old mindset. Many people worry about taxes, but in reality, the fact that you'll be paying more means that you'll be making more and contributing more. Think how your country can benefit from what you will be offering and you will see it in a different light.

Then, I have also worked with people who, as soon as they started manifesting more money, decided to fulfill their dreams of moving abroad and setting down in a country with less taxation.

Either way, this is just a limiting belief and you need to center your mindset daily to make sure you are not sabotaging your manifestation.

> Ok, so now the next step- the most important one.

5. Now that you are making 10 k a month, what does your life look like? What do you feel, hear and see?

How do you design your day?

How do you help those around you? What clothes do you wear, where do you live? How do you contribute to your society? How does it feel to make your first big manifestation come true?

Now, what you want to do is to anchor to the feeling of manifesting and detach yourself from the amount of money you want to make.

The number is just a tool to temporarily help you shift to a new reality that you now believe it will help you create.

Be as specific as possible. What food do you eat? Where, and with whom? What do you do for a living? What does your work look like? How do you relax?

So again, instead of defining yourself as a 10 k a month earner you define your reality by feelings, emotions and experiences.

Later, as we go through many fascinating success stories of people using the system from this book, you will understand why feelings are most important than numbers.

I can still remember my disappointment after doing daily journaling and affirmation with the "I am making...a month" and nothing ever happened because of that. I was just spinning my wheels and focusing on lack, not on abundance.

Now center your mindset by aligning yourself with that scenery you have just created. Do it twice a day. Ideally, you want to do it early in the morning as you are just waking up and before you go to bed.

If you are too busy, or you feel burned out because you have tried a ton of LOA rituals in the past and found yourself spinning your wheels, or maybe you just like simple solutions, you just got one.

Link your morning "feeling-visualization" practice (again both are great and if you are not a visual person, just feel it and don't worry about not being able to visualize as that puts too much stress on you and totally disconnects your manifestation).

So…link this new manifestation practice to your usual morning routine such as making and drinking coffee. I always do that.

You make your coffee and you align yourself with that new scenery you created while thinking what it would be like to double your income.

You can also hold onto that feeling on your morning shower.

Repeat in the evening.

Personally, I like to have some herbal tea and do a short meditation before I go to sleep and so I link it to my vision.

One mistake that many people make with manifesting is that they get too attached to their income goal and don't focus enough on the feelings and lifestyle they believe it will give them. There are a few dangers of that:

    -No manifestation or very slow one

-A quick spike in income and then plateau back

So, you basically do what I like to call a *quick buck manifestation* which is not bad. Everyone can do with more cash but…rather than instant or unexpected manifestations I prefer long-term secure manifestations that are deeply rooted in my vision. That allows me to make them a permanent lifestyle.

-Achieving the income goal and then getting stuck there. It happens to many entrepreneurs who start off with, "I want a 6-figure aka 10 k a month or more business". They write those goals all the time and hustle and grind.

(Now, I am not against the hard work. In fact, I work pretty hard myself, but I love what I do and it's not work at all, it's my flow and my passion… but if it kills your energy and flow and health, it can only lead to manifesting disease and anxiety rather than long-term wealth and happiness.)

Finally, they get to the desired 10 k a month. But since they programmed their minds for that number and linked so much emotions to it, they stay there.

To double their income to let's say 20 k a month using the same strategy they used before, it will take forever and will go together with lots of pain, anxiety and frustration.

I am not implying that I have a formula for some get-rich-quick manifestation or a spike. I am all for constant progress that keeps your energy where it needs to be in your particular case so that you don't burn out. That is why I always preach patience, belief and slower but constant growth and a more conservative approach compared to other LOA writers. Yes, I could manifest a quick spike in income by writing a book called *Instant Money Manifesting- Win a Lottery in 7 days or Less* but writing such a book and putting it on sale would be totally against my personal values and against my vision and would eventually turn against me.

When it comes to my teachings, I focus on long-term happiness. First, you need to set up a good foundation and re-connect with your truth. I am sure that with this book you will have many *aha* moments and discover a series of patterns that have perhaps prevented you from manifesting the fully abundant life you were meant to live.

Can you see where it's going?

You will not see me write any quick-buck manifestation book because none of these things is beneficial for the long-term (with the rare exception of someone needing money to help someone in need etc.) Then it's a different energy.

That being said- money is just paper.

So, the final step in this mindset shift and this chapter is very simple. Reconnect with the new you again, the you from another reality. The reality that already exists. The reality where you are making twice as much as money as you are making now.

At this stage you should be already detached from the number. Really, it doesn't mean anything.

Let me give you an example. A friend of mine went through this exercise. She was living on 3 k a month and her goal was 6 k a month. She kept stuck for years and she always had that 6 k or even 5 k in her mind. The way she was living was very close to poverty (according to North American standards).

She went through the exercise and saw herself with that desired income and the way she wanted to feel and live.

She wanted to wake up, do yoga and eat healthy food without worrying too much about having to save on food. Move to a sunnier part of the country where there is no depressing winter and where she could enjoy the beach. She was very specific in creating that vision and kept re-connecting herself with it twice a day just like I suggest in this book. She would even play a song with that, so it all seemed like a beautiful video she was watching on YouTube, something that really got stuck in her mind.

Finally, she completely forgot about the numbers, focused on being grateful for her humble living and had the courage to carry on doing the exercise from this chapter.

Do you know what happened? Something that had never occurred to her before. She fell in love with a man who was moving to Thailand and she moved with him. They started an online business together and now she's approaching a much bigger income than she originally wanted.

But you know what the best part is?

When she first moved to Thailand, all she had were some savings. While there, building an online business with her partner, she was able to live well and do exactly what she had intended to do in her original vision.

Wake up, do yoga, eat healthy food, swim in a nice pool and enjoy the beach. And she was doing that for only 1 k a month. That's the best part!

Before she started transforming with the methods I am sharing with you in this book, she was too fixated on that 6 k a month goal. She believed it was the only way for her to enjoy what she wanted- the yoga, healthy food, more freedom but also security, sunshine and the beach. She believed it would only happen on a holiday anyway. She manifested so much more though.

I could write an entire book filled with stories like hers which I might do if you ask me to (let me know in the review section of this book as the stories alone could be the second part).

Now this is supposed to be a short read, so I want to keep it to the point!

I hope that by now you understand how it works.

So, how to use that process to find your why? A truly compelling why.

Re-connect with that vision again. Your feelings and emotions of you making twice as much as you are making now.

This is happening right now.

Now ask yourself- *Who am I?*

Why do I DESERVE to be living it?

Answer (example):

I deserve to eat healthy food.

I deserve to live a peaceful life.

I deserve to feel aligned on the beach every day.

I deserve to be able to contribute to my community.

I deserve to be wearing nice clothes.

I deserve to be dining at nice, healthy plant-based food restaurants.

I deserve to have a personal chef.

I deserve to be a good leader.

Etc. etc.

Whatever you put on that statement is your why and the new more empowered version of yourself. It's who you are and so in alignment with it that you are already living that reality and taking actions that connect you to it.

Another why?

People you care about...

So again...re-connect with that feeling and emotion and start with:

My family deserves to travel to new countries at least twice a year.

My children deserve to eat healthy food.

Keep going! If you start crying don't worry. It's a good sign and it may actually help you get rid of some blocked emotions.

Now, that super strong and compelling why is a real why.

The real why.

Your why is not: *"Oh because I have to manifest this amount of money a month."*

That is just some illusion that will keep you away from manifesting.

So, center your mindset and emotion on your feelings and use it to re-connect with your why. Your why. You will be surprised by the results!

Mindset Shift #4 The LOA KISS Method

Honestly, most people overcomplicate LOA...and I am not judging as I have been there too. I was a victim of way too many pretty much redundant rituals that led to nothing as far as powerful manifesting goes.

Now, you already know that you can link your daily visualization and feeling practice to an already existing habit you enjoy, for example- drinking coffee or having a nice, relaxing shower or bath.

Live your experiences with your mind and already feel grateful.

In case your mind starts going with negative questions like, *What if I fail?*

Turn it around to: *What it will feel like when I succeed?*

Be aware of any negative patterns, thoughts, and circumstances as well as people that may appear in your life to test you.

Promise yourself to be stronger than that, after all... now you have your *why*. You know what is already yours and what you deserve.

Also, while it's good you share what you learn with those around you, in fact, it is my intention for you, I also recommend that you avoid sharing this process with people who are toxic or negative. Don't judge them, send them love and be kind, but make sure you protect yourself and your manifestations from negativity whether intentional or unintentional.

At the same time, if you are feeling guilty about having to hide from some people instead of being open and transparent about what you do, let me tell you this- some people come to your life for a reason, and eventually, they will learn from you.

However, the way those people will learn is through Indirect LOA Inspiration.

They will witness your transformation, and they will get inspired. They will need no words or explanations. They will then come to you and put themselves in the position of students rather than skeptics or critics.

Trust me, it happened to me many times, and each time it gets better.

At the same time that mindset shift will help you get rid of any negative emotions and the feeling of being a victim or feeling judged. (This distracts many people from abundant manifestations too).

Mindset Shift #5 The Most Powerful Word for a Bad Day (aka Your Manifestation Bridge)

What we are working on right now is your own Manifestation Bridge.

A bridge between where you are right now and where you want to go. Now, here's the thing- that bridge is you, and you need to take good care of yourself, both physically and emotionally.

At this stage, you will be put to the test on a pretty much daily basis.

There will be many negative voices in your head. Some people around you also get negative. It is now your mission to protect your vision and construct the bridge, and that bridge is the new you. The latest version of you. Stronger and more empowered.

The one word you need to remind yourself of whenever feeling you're are sliding down to the path of self-pity, guilt or any negativity is *Courage*.

I have that word written down on my vision board, and I have a courage card in my wallet. It's also a background for my phone and computer. I get reminded of that word many, many times. *Courage. Courage. Courage.*

You need that courage to create that great bridge and be able to repeat the process so that you are continually moving to new levels of manifestations.

The first times are always a bit harder, and there are more fears and doubts. Your old self will try to fight it back.

You see, I won't lie to you, we are our own biggest obstacles when it comes to our manifestations. I was, yet I was blaming everyone else (more about that later).

Manifestation is not a linear process. All you need to be doing is continually aligning yourself with the feeling and emotion of your vision. The feeling can be backed up by affirmations, journaling, and meditations as well as visualizations. But these are just tools. You already know that your vision and the emotion you attach to it is the most potent thing you need to focus on.

In fact, sometimes you need to go back to this very first step in this process.

Then there is also patience. Whenever you are getting impatient make sure to re-align yourself to the feeling of your vision.

And the best part is: going through those feelings with a smile on your face is what helps you manifest for the long-term.

Courage, courage, courage.

Remember my friend? The one who was making 3 k a month and had a "goal" of 6 k a month?

By the way, the money income goal is now out because we know that it's just a number and a part of setting up the initial process of reconnecting to your vision and emotion.

So, as you already know my friend was going through the practices and methods described in this book.

And she had that particular freedom-sunshine vision, right?

On a conscious and linear level, if someone had asked her back then, "OK, so how do you think you can earn more money?" She would have said, "Well, get a better job. Maybe invest in my education so that I can get a better job. Maybe learn about creating my own business. Or keep my job and start a side business to make more income. Or maybe, win the lottery, or perhaps some unknown relative leaves me money."

These were all that I like to call *conscious clues*, and while these are all legitimate vehicles to earn income, the best way that will be your ultimate and long-term manifestation that will really change your life is never that simple to express.

It appears eventually after going through the initial *Build the Bridge Phase*.

One of the crucial elements is what I like to call *The Taste of Manifestation*.

Let me give you an example because at this stage it's probable you may not be following me, and I don't blame you for that.

That information may be hard to swallow at first.

My friend followed precisely what I am teaching in this book. She created a vision that would make her happy and kept aligned and re-connected with that vision, twice a day. Morning and evening. Also, she did it very often during the day too as she was so excited about it. At the same time, she kept saying the word *courage* whenever negative thoughts would sweep in, and this would help her shift from frustration to gratitude and from fear to courage.

At that time, she didn't know that within one year she would be in another country, living her dream life on less money and in addition to that living with the man of her dreams. (He came as another manifestation due to her being courageous as you will soon find out.)

And…she could never have expected that within two years of her getting started with this process she would be running an online business, together with her partner. A company that eventually took them to multiple six figures. She had no idea about those opportunities back then, but one thing would lead to the next.

I call it *the LOA Domino Effect*. I love it.

You see, you need to pay close attention to what is happening around you. The best way to do it is to start testing your dream reality. Why? It's like a test drive. During those tests, as you examine your dream reality while still in your old one, your state and emotional wellbeing shift even more, and you start attracting what I like to call *Powerful Manifestation Messengers*.

Now, those messengers may be ordinary people who don't feel like they are on a mission. For them, they are in their default reality doing their own thing. But the Universe aligns them with you for a reason.

My friend spent the initial three months with no significant changes or manifestations in her life.

Still, she religiously stuck to the process I have described earlier in this book and also in this chapter.

She was still technically at the same income level. But deep inside she already believed and felt her new reality and felt ready to test it. At the same time, she completely detached herself from her income goal and focused on her feelings instead.

Please note - I am not saying you should forget about the money, stop paying your bills or don't file your taxes. Needless to say, because of the dimension we live in, you need to keep an eye on that.

I am referring to your emotions and to your emotional attachment to numbers. In most people that attachment is not healthy because it comes from a place of scarcity, lack, and insecurity.

I am not good enough now at my current income. But when I manifest this level, then I will be good, and everyone will love me for it.

That is a dead end, my friend. It's a vicious cycle that will never lead to fulfillment. What happens then is endless hustle, fear, and scarcity.

So back to our friend. She knew she had to taste her ideal reality. To do that, she decided to go for a quick solo trip for a few days to the south of the country and enjoy the beach.

At first, she came up with an excuse:

Man, I can't afford it. It's expensive. Yeah, I can get another job or extra shifts at work, but then I will run out of money.

Luckily, she quickly reminded herself of *Courage*.

And so, for a few weeks, she took an extra job as a babysitter and saved up money to be able to go on her short solo trip, taste the sunshine, beach and healthy food and participate in a yoga workshop.

Many of her family and friends thought she was crazy.

"If your goal is to make more money, it's better for you to save that money and use it for a college or certification so that you can later get a better job." This was the most common advice from family and friends.

That was also what she heard in her head and was stuck with for an extended period. She tried that route before. She'd tried different professional courses yet could never find the passion or fulfillment she needed to keep her going.

"Stop wasting money on travel. It's almost Christmas, can you afford to waste so much money now?" her mom kept saying.

But...My friend kept saying to herself, *Courage. Courage. Courage.*

Don't get me wrong. Her family and friends were worried about her and were giving her a piece of solid advice that they believed was the best. And yeah, it makes sense if you employ a linear way of thinking. *I need this to get this and that to go there and then I will be happy, whole and complete.* (Very often it doesn't end that well even if a person manages to earn the desired income level. It usually ends with burnout, some chronic disease or anxiety that take at least a few years of intense work to heal.)

Ok, back to my friend, off she went to the south and guess what?

It was there that she met her partner. Love at first sight.

A few months after, they both moved to Thailand. After tasting her dream reality, the *Manifestation Messenger* appeared. (In her case, it was her true love). I always tell her that was like a second manifestation.

Maybe it was because of all the courage she put in at the beginning?

You already know how the story ends. By totally immersing herself in her dream reality (even though at first her income dropped because she quit her job and lived off her savings and while in Thailand teaching English to make some money). But it was a temporary "sacrifice." Giving up the old to be ready for the new.

I use inverted commas for the word "sacrifice" because again, amongst us "manifesters" it's not really a sacrifice, but someone coming from a linear world would not get it.

If your goal is 6 k and your job pays you 3 k, and now you quit, how will you ever reach that goal?

Goal. Hustle. Attachment. Strong emotional attachment and carrying too much of other people's opinions.

Also, please note, this is an unusual story. And yes, a person with children and family obligations may not be able to move overseas. That is not the point of this chapter. That story simply illustrates an example, and everyone is different and will have a different story.

By being courageous and sticking to your vision that you already know is yours and then really feeling it, you feel ready and entirely worthy and deserving to taste your dream reality even before you are prepared.

From there, you attract *Manifestation Messengers*. In some cases, they are not people but simply circumstances (and in some cases, they may be perceived as bad, for example losing your job may lead you to get a new better one or changing your career while aligning yourself with your passion).

Still, the *Manifestation Messengers'* goal is to show you the new reality you deserve and make sure you get there as soon as possible.

Another example- another friend of mine had a goal of making a certain amount of money that would allow him to have a nice sports car. He just loves cars.

He had this vision. He drives a car with his wife they go to beautiful places together, and he feels sunshine on him. Again, he was living in a pretty cold part of the country. For years he "tried to be successful" and "do whatever it took" and "hustle" to get that dream car.

In reality, it wasn't just about the car. He wanted to feel free, be creative, live in a warm climate and have a job that would give him the flexibility of time to spend with his wife.

He worked in the software development department of a big company that always kept him on the brink of getting that promotion. Yet something would always happen, and they would give it to someone else. He worked harder and harder. Long hours and business trips that felt very lonely. He did not feel worthy or appreciated and felt envious of guys who not only had a nice car but also had time to enjoy it with family and friends.

When he came to me for help, he was on the brink of an emotional breakdown. Still, we worked through the process and created his vision. Because of his technical, logical background at first he had difficulty with focusing on his feelings and emotions.

Eventually, he was able to allow the manifestation flow to kick in and just feel courageous. He gave up linear thinking altogether.

It turned out that his technical career did not excite him at all. Years ago, he had chosen that route as he felt he could get a secure engineering job and make his dad happy.

What he was passionate about was creativity, marketing, organizing events, having fun while meeting new people. He also really enjoyed writing, and that was a helpful tool for him to reconnect with his vision. I have noticed that different people prefer different tools. Some like to sit and visualize, some want to sit and write out their vision every day, in the present tense and feel grateful for it. Some people like affirmations.

Some people go hardcore and do all the techniques. Which can be great if it's done from a place of passion, joy, and curiosity but never works if a person does it because they feel impatient and want to desperately speed up the whole process to impress themselves or other people.

Back to my friend. He religiously kept going through the simple *reconnect to your vision* exercise, morning and evening.

Eventually, he felt ready to taste his dream reality.

He took his family on a short vacation to the sunny south and rented his dream car for taste rides.

One of those rides led him to meet someone who invited him to a business conference. At that conference he met the CEO of a very creative marketing company where they were looking for someone with software development experience to help them develop a new product.

He took that job which led him to move to a more beautiful, sunnier city. In his new career he felt much more appreciated although the pay was a bit lower at first than in his old job.

Still, he was already testing his new reality.

The new company he worked for really admired his dedication and work ethic as well as other talents and skills he demonstrated outside of his primary field of expertise. Now he's an Executive Marketing Director, and aside from an excellent salary and benefits he also has a company car. This is what happens when you abandon linear thinking and understand that long-term manifestations do require some courage and sincere belief.

The initial transformation may also require some sacrifice and the leaving of your comfort zone.

Now, this is a taboo topic among most LOA teachers and writers. Honestly, though, the old model where you just focus on the techniques (meditate, visualize, affirm) without getting to the root of the problem is not effective at all. It's all about understanding why you want what you want. Then you can focus on the feeling and the root (the reason why you really want something) and you transcend the desire with peace of mind. That peace of mind comes from knowing that what you want is already yours.

For example, I am writing this book, and in my writing, I may go against some societal norms or even what many LOA gurus or writers teach. That requires courage. I know that someone may send me a hate email. This has happened before and probably will happen again. But I don't focus on that. Instead, I reconnect with the feeling of joy and happiness I get whenever I get a *thank you* email or review from a happy reader. That feeling helps me overcome a bad day when perhaps I don't feel like writing.

Yet I drink my coffee, I reconnect with that feeling, I meditate, or if I happen to travel, I just have my coffee on the beach and then write from a coffee shop or a hotel.

When I am on that track, I can already taste my New Reality. In this case, it's the new reality of the creation I am bringing to life which is this book.

I am not focusing on what could go wrong. That would stop me from taking meaningful action. Instead, I keep aligning myself with my vision and my new book is also getting aligned with its original vision and mission. I think of it as a separate entity that I am teaching this process to even though it's my creation.

However, to create it, and to enjoy the process, I need to take care of my energy and detach myself from the vanity of metrics and numbers.

Last week someone wrote to me and asked me how to launch a bestselling book with a certain number of reviews.

I politely replied that it's never been my goal. When writing, I focus on creating value for my readers. I detach myself from the time too. I don't stress out about writing less on a given day. When I write- I write, and it flows. Some days I write more and, on some days, less. I do not impose any artificial goals and get stressed out about all those vanity metrics.

Of course, these are vanity metrics for me. Other people may genuinely enjoy setting their own goals in their own ways and aim to have a certain number of ratings and reviews on their book's page. Maybe they want to write a certain number of words each day and stick to that. That's fine if it suits them. My goal here is not to judge.

Your manifestation starts with your awareness. Ask yourself, are you too busy with the linear process and vanity metrics? Can you really align with them? Where do they actually lead you?

Finally, I highly recommend you do what my friends did:

1. Center your mindset daily, preferably twice a day, by focusing on your feelings, that is, the feeling you get when you align with your vision.
2. Ask yourself- what can you do to taste your new reality right here right now? Treat it as a temporary mini manifestation that is entirely under your control. Some people may call you crazy, that's fine, it's their opinion, opinions are not objective. Stay aligned with your vision.
3. When you do allow yourself the taste of your dream reality, it's quite possible you will come across your

Manifestation Messenger or *Messengers*. In some cases, they may manifest as objects, circumstances, animals, or something you will merely feel is a sign.

In some cases, it may be even something that always happens, yet you never valued it or never perceived it as your *Manifestation Messenger*.

Tasting your dream really is a fantastic step, and there is no reason you should deprive yourself of it.

Get back to the earlier pages of this book and read the inspiring stories of my friends and clients if you need to. At this stage, though, you should focus on yourself, your long-term vision and ultimate manifestation.

Mindset Shift #6 Own Yourself

When it comes to manifesting, most people focus on what they want to manifest and how to go about it.

However, the most often overlooked point is – *what place are they manifesting from?*

What about you? What place are you manifesting from?

A place of abundance or scarcity?

A place of confidence or fear?

A place where you are already feeling whole and complete or one of "*I will be happy when…*"?

For me, personally, it was a big pill to swallow. I used to feel like a victim all the time. Whatever happened to me, it was always someone else's fault.

It felt more comfortable and, as the years went by, I became addicted to feeling like a victim. It became my pattern. I would apply that pattern all the time to all areas of my life.

I would sabotage my health thinking, "Yeah, I may try this diet but what's the point if in my family everyone puts on weight easily?

And yeah, I had hypnosis for weight loss, some healthy cookbooks, a ton of meal plans, a gym membership and more guided hypnosis. I was thinking I was doing everything, and I would even brag that I take the holistic approach. But it did not work, so I blamed my family and their genes and also the creators of the books and courses I purchased.

It was only when I realized that I was in a victim mindset and decided to switch to an owner mindset that I was able to transform. I suddenly felt grateful for all the years I had been overweight because they had allowed me to understand and shift my victim mindset and create a grateful owner mindset instead.

I know people who have been through much more pain, rejection and suffering in their lives than I have.

Yet they have managed to turn that suffering into something meaningful, something that helps other people and at the same time helps them become abundant creators and owners.

I was also a victim in my relationship, and it was always someone else's fault. And yeah...if you have ever been in an abusive relationship, I know how you feel right now. I totally understand it's hard. The thing is, you may technically be a victim, but you can choose to be an owner instead. Whatever happened to you happened for a reason. You can transform it into something positive. The book I would recommend for this matter is *Man's Search for Meaning* by Viktor E. Frankl.

Now back to manifesting money and abundance...why do you need to switch from a victim mindset to an owner mindset?

As Tony Robbins once said, "Life doesn't happen *to* you it happens *for* you."

Challenge yourself every day to center your mindset around it. Whenever you find yourself thinking- why is it taking so long, why am I not manifesting yet? Why am I always stuck in a traffic jam, why this and that, ask yourself- why is it happening for me? What is it trying to tell me?

Oh, yeah, it's taking so long because I am supposed to master the process. Makes sense. Actually, I am grateful for that. I will master the process. I am learning.

Traffic jam? Ah, right, it's a sign that I need to start waking up earlier. I was thinking of allowing myself to go through a fantastic LOA morning ritual where I can meditate, align with my vision, workout to lift my energy and vibration and even make a healthy plant-based breakfast. I can be up early, leave for work early, be at work early, and when I am there I can inspire others and attract new opportunities.

I have a friend who started doing that after changing his perception of traffic jams and thanks to that he got a promotion and a pay rise. The boss was on the fence about choosing him or somebody else, but the other person kept coming in late and blaming traffic jams.

My friend would be ahead of time and ready to shoot off and work with full focus at 9 AM when the work would start.

Promotion led him not only to get a pay rise but also learning new skills. Eventually, he quit his job to start his own business with his own team. He now successfully leads that team, and the business he has is much more aligned with his passion than his old job.

While in the job he was grateful and showed up ahead of time and set an example to other colleagues. He stuck to his rules. He also discovered that he had so much more energy after waking up earlier.

Look, if you're like me and you were born into a poor family, don't feel like a victim. It's your advantage and competitive edge. You are the owner.

You are a fantastic human being and thanks to whatever happened to you, you feel stronger and more aligned with your vision. Be grateful for your past. It led you to where you are now and on this journey of amazing self-development. Right now, you are reading this book because of the reason. That reason is whatever happened to you made you who you are (or who you're becoming). Had your life always been perfect you would not have bothered to progress and develop your consciousness and awareness.

To finish off this chapter ask yourself:

When do I feel like a victim? Has feeling like a victim prevented me from manifesting in the past?

How can I shift to the owner mindset today?

Be aware of what thoughts you are thinking. Reframe them. That will allow you to stay stronger and more aligned with your vision.

The suffering was just a little step to make you stronger. It was just a test. You are on a long-term manifestation journey- remember that!

And let me quote Tony Robbins again: "Life doesn't happen *to* you, it happens *for* you".

In case you still feel like a victim or find it hard to get rid of negative addictive emotions and thoughts I would recommend you check out Dr. Joe Dispenza's books and meditations. They helped me tremendously.

The exercise for this step is to write down all the situations where you have felt like a victim. Then, rewrite them in a more powerful way. First, focus on some experience from the past and then move on to your current situation and the circumstances that you feel may be blocking you right now.

Example:

Old belief:

I got fired from my job.

I had to degrade my lifestyle.

I felt horrible. I mean who does that? I studied hard and I worked hard.

All companies are the same. They don't care about human beings.

New belief:

Losing my job was the best thing that ever happened to me.

I got inspired to change my career, and in between even though I had to degrade my lifestyle and went through some financial difficulties, I found myself with lots of free time.

I used that time to focus on my passion and align myself with my new vision.

This eventually led me to get a new job, and I manifested some unexpected commissions.

It did happen for me, and I am so thankful.

Old victim belief:

All men/women are the same. I gave it my all in my last relationship. I gave up my family and friends, and I completely changed my lifestyle and schedule to fit in my ex-partner's. I can't believe he/she left me. Who does that? They did not appreciate me at all.

New empowering belief:

At first, it was hard to understand why my ex-partner broke up with me but eventually it led me to learn a ton of things about myself.

Yes, the initial break up stage was hard, but it inspired me to re-connect with some old friends, and I also began working with a therapist. I now understand that I can't sacrifice my own happiness to make other people happy. I felt like it happened to me for a reason and I am so grateful for it.

Now I am in a fantastic relationship, and I communicate better while making sure there is a healthy balance, and nobody feels like a victim. Full trust.

Oh, and congrats! You are halfway through, and the rest of the steps in this manifestation method will be shorter and more straightforward.

The first part of the book was definitely the most challenging one, and it's where you were supposed to experience the greatest number of breakthroughs.

However, if you are still feeling like you may be lacking clarity for your plan of action, I recommend you re-read all the previous steps.

Mindset Shift #7 The Resourceful Method

The best manifestation success story from this book is the double manifestation my friend experienced. Not only money but also the love of her life.

However, to get where she got, she had to be resourceful. For example, she wanted to test her dream reality by making a short solo trip to the south of the country, and she had no money for that.

Well, what she did was to offer a cleaning service in her area. It wasn't the best long-term solution, and she had to use her spare time to clean other people's houses to be able to afford that dream trip.

However, as she was going through that process, she felt happy, grateful, aligned and centered. A few days after her doing two jobs, she manifested a mini bonus payment from her main job, which was the first time it had ever happened at the company she worked for.

Those things always take place when you are grateful, center your mindset daily and commit yourself to be resourceful. That means no moaning and no complaining!

You already know that EVERYTHING happens for you, not to you.

You already know that the opportunity is abundant.

So now, it's your turn. How resourceful are you?

What are you willing to sacrifice?

Do you feel like you may be wasting your time on activities that do not align with your vision?

Do you feel like there are certain activities that even though are not super-sexy at first glance, may help you get closer to your vision, or can help you to test your dream reality faster?

Are you willing to accept certain temporary sacrifices while enjoying them, with a smile on your face?

Remember- it all happens *for* you. The opportunities around us are very abundant and have always been that way. The problem is when we overcomplicate things with our conscious, analytical minds. It's time to say *no* to that craziness and negativity and focus on your manifestations.

In my case, for example, I knew I wanted to work with a mindset coach, and I had to invest some money in his coaching.

You already know what my situation was.... broke.

But I knew I needed his guidance to help me break through my own limitations and I just had the feeling that this was the missing part on my journey. I spent a weekend with a pen and notebook looking for ideas to generate extra income.

Here's what I did:

-I sold some old items on eBay.

-I organized a small workshop for children, teaching drawing (everyone has something they can teach in their local community).

-I offered a simple design service online.

-I offered a few Spanish classes to a friend who was moving to Spain and needed to polish up his Spanish.

While none of those mini side jobs made me manifest large amounts of money, they allowed me to gather some side income and focus on my next step which was deep inner work with a coach.

I did not moan or complain like I surely would have before I began experiencing my transformation.

Plus, I genuinely enjoyed all those mini jobs and felt good about offering a quality service. I did not care at all about what other people were saying: "Elena is losing her mind. She is now unemployed, and obviously she can't find a real job anywhere."

I just focused on what made sense to me. Again, opportunities are abundant. When you stay aligned with your vision, going through temporary sacrifices makes total sense.

And you know what? This is REAL gratitude. You stay in motion, and you move forward. You show up. You also show the Universe that you are committed, and that you really want to taste your dream reality while at the same time having faith in the Universe to offer you the best solution for your situation.

Now it's your turn. How can you move to a more resourceful mindset?

And, most importantly, how can you become more aware of the situations where you give up or complain and become a resourceful manifestor instead?

Mindset Shift #8 Your LOA Stamina to Keep Believing & Achieving

Those who don't manifest give up too soon.

I know it's harsh...but any investment takes time and so does re-programming your mind.

What I recommend you focus on at this stage of your journey are even more alignment exercises. Stay aligned with your vision and that feeling. It's already happening. Right here. Right now.

Set a series of reminders on your phone and use them to re-connect with your big vision at least a few times a day.

Long-term manifestations do take time and consist of a meaningful combo of the law of attraction with the law of action.

Do not allow anyone to distract you. You need to stay extremely focused, and it's thanks to the focus that you will be able to develop what I like to call your LOA muscle, and that is amazing.

It's one of the intentions I have for you. I want you to master the process and feel confident about it.

As an exercise for this short chapter, I highly recommend that you do the following:

Ask yourself, when was the last time you really wanted something to manifest but eventually since it was taking more time than you originally envisioned, you decided to quit? Or maybe, you were even feeling like, *that may not be for me.*

Remember, you are a remarkable human being. Never ever allow yourself to settle for less than you can be, do or have.

Your potential is unlimited. To fully unleash it you need time and clarity. If you already know what you want and have a vision you can align to via your feelings, emotions and actions, not by some meaningless numbers, vanity goals or empty promises, then you are already on your way to manifesting whatever you want.

Any challenges and obstacles are just a test created by the Universe to, first, see if you really want what you are asking for. It's also a LOA gym to help you grow that LOA muscle. That way, next time you can create an unlimited manifestation momentum that will create real miracles in your life.

Another thing I recommend you do is to start asking the Universe for patience. Do it at least a few times a day. Ask for endurance, energy, and strength. That is the sign of alignment, surrender and a deep belief. At the same time, be sure to take this action from a place of abundance and confidence, not from a place of a scarcity. Don't be like, "I am not good enough SOS Universe do something for me ASAP".

Make sense?

Talking about an abundance mindset- it's the next chapter.

Mindset Shift #9 Abundant Mindset Mastery

How do you feel when you spend money?

For example, when you pay for a car repair, or pay your bills or buy food. Do you feel like, "Heck, why is it getting more and more expensive?"

If that's you, it's time to change this mindset.

From now on, whenever you pay for something, whether it's paid by cash, credit card, bank transfer or any other means, on or offline, swap the feeling of scarcity with the sense of gratitude.

"Wow, it's great I can just buy food. It saves my time. It's great I can buy clothes, I wouldn't even know how to make my own. Oh, and I am so grateful I just paid the water and electricity bill. Thanks to that I can live in a comfortable way. Many people on this planet can't even experience such a luxury so why would I complain about it?"

Exercise 1- go through the same process yourself.

Remind yourself of at least three situations where you recently spent money, even on some basic stuff. Now ask yourself how you can be grateful for that while practicing an abundance mindset.

Here's another mindset shift. From now on, it's absolutely prohibited for you to say, "I can't afford it." Now, you only want to say, "How can I afford it?" The best part is that now we will re-modify the first exercise and practice gratitude for the items, objects, and experiences we haven't technically purchased yet.

Exercise #2

Think of three random items or experiences (for example, some trips) that you currently want.

Imagine that you buy them, pay for them, feel the money or the credit card in your hand and be grateful. Feel it.

Now make sure you add that feeling to your daily alignment that you know is the best practice you can focus on, at least twice a day.

Finally, ask yourself- how are you taking action? Is it from a place of abundance or scarcity? For example, my friend took a second job cleaning people's houses, but she did it from a place of absolute bliss and abundance. She not only felt grateful as she was getting paid that extra money that allowed her to go on a short vacation and unexpectedly manifest the man of her dreams. She also felt grateful while doing the job. Again, it wasn't her passion, but she knew it was a part of the process.

You can be always passionate about the process, accept it and surrender to it fully while taking inspired action from a place of abundance.

She did not take action from a place of being a victim, saying, "I am a loser. I's not fair that I need to work two jobs to be able to go on a holiday. It's not my fault that the university is so expensive. My parents could never afford to pay for my education. I can't believe my wages are so low I need another job."

Can you see a difference? How does that apply to your situation?

Are you taking action from a place of abundance or scarcity?

Whatever LOA practice you are doing...are you acting from a place of abundance or scarcity?

Remember- you are good enough now. Make sure you re-write all your story right here right now to make sure you are taking action from a place of abundance.

Fill in the gaps:

I ....am feeling whole and complete right here right now.

I take meaningful action from a place of abundance.

I deserve to live an abundant life.

Life happens for me, not to me.

I am grateful and proactive. I am and so I can. I unleash my full potential.

Money is abundant and whenever I have the opportunity to offer cash for someone's product or service, I feel aligned with my vision and ultimate joy.

Enjoy this one, it's a real game changer!

Mindset Shift #10 Be on the Other Side

Give, give, give and be kind while giving.

That one used to be very challenging for me. I had those voices in my head...*Elena, how can you give more if you don't have enough yourself? You're on the verge of going on unemployment benefits. It's scary...*

Yes, it was, but I did not let that feeling get me off my vision. First, I looked at some items I had around the house, some things I could just donate to a charity. Then I decided to create a simple micro habit and started giving money to causes I wanted to support. Whenever I could do that, I felt so grateful.

As Bob Proctor says, "Money must circulate."

I wholeheartedly agree with that statement. The more you give, the more you receive. By giving you are sending out a signal to the Universe that you are already feeling whole, complete and abundant and are no longer on a scarcity vibration.

While you don't have to donate everything you have got, be sure to assign a certain amount of money, weekly and monthly and stick to it. As you start making more money- raise it. For best results, be sure to combine your donations with random acts of kindness. Do something to put a smile on other people's faces. Right now, you are stepping into the higher, and more divine version of you. You will feel like a different person.

What you can also do is take some spare food or make sandwiches and give the food away to your local homeless shelter or give it away to the homeless people you may encounter on the streets. Never stop giving. When you stop giving you stop receiving.

Be proactive. There is always a way to give something to someone even if right now you cannot do it directly by sending money to someone. Just focus on the abundance mindset and ask yourself how you can be a better giver.

Add it to your prayers. Now you ask the Universe for energy, patience, focus and you also ask how to be a better giver. Enjoy!

Mindset Shift #11 The Invisible Force That Makes You Fail or Succeed (and how to use it to manifest what you want)

Aside from the word *courage* I warmly invite you to get into an empowering habit of repeating *I can, I am* as often as you can.

You see, the manifestation process is connected to your self-image. If deep inside you think that wealth and abundance are not for you, you will not be able to attract what you want. Luckily there are certain mindsets and even lifestyle exercises you can start applying to help you transform your self-image:

-Keep reminding yourself of *I can, I am* throughout the day.

-Remember that you are already feeling whole and complete.

- Consciously decide to do things differently as if you were a new person. Go to a party you usually wouldn't go to. Do your hair differently.

-Every day look yourself in the mirror and remind yourself of how grateful you are to be you.

Finally, take a piece of paper, or use your LOA journal and write down your name with 2_0 next to it.

Example: Elena 2_0

Now, re-connect with your vision. Get into that fantastic feeling because the reality you want to manifest already exists.

Now ask yourself- *Who am I in that new reality*? Have an objective look at the new You. Imagine you are a stranger and look at the new, transformed version of yourself.

How do you behave? What do you wear? Who do you hang out with? What do you eat? Where do you live? Where do you travel?

Now ask yourself- *What action can I take to fuse myself with that new, more empowered version of myself?* Right now, you are getting closer and closer to the art of meaningful manifestations. You are moving way beyond your current reality and massively increasing your vibration by merely changing your mindset and tuning into your feelings and emotions. You are transcending your old self and your old reality. As you keep going through these steps, you may attract more *Manifestation Messengers*. Things will be different. By aligning yourself with the new more empowered version of yourself, you are experiencing similar heights as when tasting your dream reality. Enjoy!

Mindset Shift #12 Your Net Worth Starts with Self-Worth

Please note that this step may be a bit uncomfortable, especially if you are like me and you are coming from a poor family where money was scarce, and everyone would always look for the cheapest option out there and the most discount.

If that is your case, it may take some time to go through it. But here's what you need to understand: your buying behaviors will always reflect in your money attracting abilities.

I know, I know, you are probably wondering- *But Elena, what must I do if I am really broke right now? How can I afford to buy more expensive items instead of living on the cheapest things possible?*

It's simple. If that's your case, create just one simple ritual. For example, allow yourself that once a week, or once a month, you will break away from old patterns and buy a more expensive item, just to experience the feeling of being a premium customer.

When you do that, get back to the abundance mindset and think- *Wow, someone on the other side had a fantastic money manifestation idea and they are not afraid to charge higher prices.*

I used to work with an entrepreneur who came to me feeling very frustrated about his business. He said that everyone in his industry would do better than him even though he would always charge the lowest prices possible. His goal, however, was to have premium clients.

After having some deep conversations with him, I realized that he was still afraid of money. Then I asked him, "How much would you like to charge your clients?"

He said, "5 k for a full package service I am offering."

And I wondered, "Have you ever invested 5 k in a similar service?"

He said, "No." At the same time, he was looking for sales and marketing "hacks" to learn how to attract more money to his business. Yet...nothing would happen.

Finally, he decided to change his buying behaviors and started experiencing the feeling of an abundant, premium client. That helped him get into the mindset of wealthy people, and what they really value in a service he was offering. That one simple action changed him, and he totally re-designed his business.

"Oh," someone might say, "that's not fair, how come he only wants to serve wealthy clients?"

Well, aside from his business he also runs his own charity helping hungry kids. He's in the cycle of giving and receiving. He understands the game by now.

Now, I hope that you have gotten a simple yet profound understanding of how LOA, mindset, and self-image can work together to help you manifest more wealth and abundance by getting to the root of the problem and helping you transform on a deeper level.

As a final exercise ask yourself:

"How do I react when I see higher prices? Do I judge and criticize people who set them up for people who pay them? Do I think I am smarter for always spending my time looking for the cheapest items possible?"

Again, there is nothing wrong with that at all if that is your choice.

If you are driven by scarcity however deep inside you would like to be free to buy whatever you want without checking the price tags and at the same time you judge and criticize people who love to order premium products and services …well chances are you are sending out a very misleading vibrations to the Universe which may result in you feeling stuck for years.

How do I know? Because I have been there too, and it took me years of LOA, mindset and deep self-development work to re-create my beliefs and start aligning myself with abundance.

It is my intention that you do the same while enjoying peace, freedom, and fulfillment.

I believe in you. You are a fantastic human being. I am here to support you. In case you want to get in touch with me, you will find more information on the following pages.

Before you go...

Before you go, I need your help. It will only take a few minutes of your precious time. If you enjoyed this book could you please leave me a short review on Amazon?

Many people in our community will benefit from your review, and it may even inspire them to start practicing the deep transformative LOA techniques described in this book.

Thanks in advance!

PS. All my books are also available in audiobook format.

You will find them at:

www.loaforsuccess.com/audiobooks

A Special Offer from Elena to Help You Manifest Faster.

Finally, I would like to invite you to join my private mailing list (my **VIP LOA Newsletter**). Whenever I release a new book, you will be able to get it at a discounted price (or sometimes even for free, but don't tell anyone 😉).

In the meantime, I will keep you entertained with a free copy of my exclusive LOA workbook that will be emailed to you when you sign up.

To join visit the link below now:

www.loaforsuccess.com/newsletter

After you have signed up, you will get a free instant access to this exclusive workbook (+ many other helpful resources that I will be sending you on a regular basis). I hope you will enjoy your free workbook.

If you have any questions, please email us at: support@loaforsuccess.com

More Books written by Elena G.Rivers

Available at: www.loaforsuccess.com

Ebook – Paperback – Audiobook Editions Available Now

Law of Attraction for Amazing Relationships

Law of Attraction for Weight Loss

Law of Attraction for Abundance

Law of Attraction Manifestation Exercises

You will find more at:

www.loaforsuccess.com/books

www.ingramcontent.com/pod-product-compliance
Lightning Source LLC
Chambersburg PA
CBHW071020080526
44587CB00015B/2429